# From Margaritas to Mac 'n Cheese Mom

Keeping your humor, losing your sanity, and embracing the journey

By Deborah Stumm

Copyright © 2012 Deborah Stumm

All rights reserved. This book, or parts thereof, may not be reproduced in any form without written permission.

ISBN: 0615597017
ISBN-13: 9780615597010
Library of Congress Control Number: 2012903615
From Margaritas to Mac 'n Cheese Mom, San Diego, CA

Cover image by Amanda Rhett
Author photo by Nick Biliotti

For more information or quantity sales,
visit SuperMoms360.com

# To

Morgan and Dylan, my amazing kids who have given me a new reason to be my best every day.

My husband, Mark, who doesn't really understand this book (since he's not a mom) but has been patient and supportive during the entire journey.

My parents, who are still married after forty-seven years and have given me the ultimate gift of family and instilled the importance of perseverance.

The amazing women that have been put in my path—who have inspired me to embrace my individuality and pushed me to go further than I ever knew I could go.

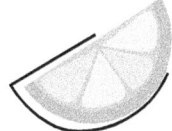

# Forward

**"Life isn't about finding yourself,
it's about creating yourself."**
– Author unknown

As a general rule, I'm not a big fan of motivational quotes. This particular statement, however, jumped out at me from a coffee mug that was sitting on the shelf at my local coffee shop. The simple concept grabbed me, and I actually purchased the mug so I wouldn't forget it. This seemingly small life moment became significant because I was in the midst of a huge transition in my life—the journey from independent single woman to becoming a wife and mother.

The idea for this book came because there have been many points in my evolution from singlehood to "super mom" when I have wondered, "What happened to me?" I *used to be* young, fun, hip, spontaneous, and successful, and now I'm a soccer mom, class party mom, and most importantly, Morgan and Dylan's mom. Well, I may not be quite as young anymore (*sigh*), but I've realized that it *is* possible to stay true to yourself in mommyhood if you allow yourself to embrace the journey.

When I find myself starting to forget who I really am, it seems that I just need to look to my spirited children to help find my way back. On a busy Tuesday night, after dinner and homework were done, my son (age six), daughter (age seven), and I made our way to the living room for our weekly dance party. My husband, who is not a fan of this ritual, added his normal response of a grunt followed by a quick escape to his "man cave" upstairs.

With the boom box playing and the three of us grooving, we bonded over some Justin Bieber and Katy Perry tunes. Morgan, who is...shall we say...*not* a classically trained dancer, looked up at me with sheer joy and said, "Mom, do you know how I got to be such an *incredible* dancer? I just turn off my brain, and *let it go!*" In that moment, which was a mixture of hilarity and clarity, I realized that my seven-year-old might be onto something.

Accepting ourselves as we are is something we often forget. As we go through life, we begin to worry about always doing the right thing, acting the right way, and pleasing everyone—except maybe ourselves. This book, at its core, is about acceptance. It's about embracing our imperfections and our strengths—and the fact that we sometimes need to ask for help.

# How to Read This Book

First things first. This is an imperfect book written by an imperfect mom. It's not intended to be a know-it-all instruction manual. It's a *real* book for *real* moms that acknowledges that we all struggle to keep our sanity and identity on our quest to be better moms, wives, and especially individuals. It's not one-size-fits-all, so feel free to take things or leave them as you see fit.

Each chapter focuses on an area that I've found to be especially helpful during my own personal process. There have been numerous times I've doubted my individuality and failed to acknowledge the value of my own uniqueness. I hope you find this to be a fresh approach to the daily struggle that we as moms face as we embrace motherhood while trying to maintain ourselves at the core.

# How Did I Get Here?

It's hard to remember what it was like to be single. Before my husband, before my kids. What did I do with all of my time? I'm a bit nostalgic for my Manhattan Beach cottage that was just steps from the sand, my high-powered job that had me traveling the world, staying up late, and sleeping in on the weekends. At the time, I remember thinking that I would never meet "the one" and had pretty much resigned myself to the idea that I would always be single and never have kids of my own. I convinced myself that this was okay, but I knew it wasn't. Even in the midst of my margarita-drinking, convertible-driving, and beach-going days, I had a deep desire to be a mom.

People always ask, "How did you and your husband meet?" There are two versions of the story: the rated G version and the *real* story. For my kids (and my parents), the story goes that Mommy and Daddy met in Palm Springs. Daddy was on a golf weekend with the boys, and Mommy was visiting with her friends. In actuality, we met in a super-cheesy nightclub (which *was* in Palm Springs for the record), and I "picked up" my now husband. I couldn't help it; he was gorgeous, and he also wasn't paying the least bit of attention to me. After a few Ketel One and cranberries (I lost count), and an evening of tearing up the dance floor, he walked me to my room. No, I didn't invite him in, and I can't believe you would even think that!

We began our whirlwind romance with me in the Los Angeles area and he in San Diego. We were both extremely independent and stuck in our ways, so it worked for a while. Eventually, though, we knew that one of us would need to move.

It was Easter morning, and Mark and I were visiting my family in the San Francisco Bay Area. As usual, my parents insisted on having our annual Easter egg hunt. At thirty-one, I was a little perturbed by the ritual that I had obviously outgrown. I decided not to make a fuss and happily (not really) hopped around the backyard collecting plastic eggs. When it came time to open our loot, I boasted to my family that I had found the biggest egg in the yard—the purple egg. When I cracked it open, my engagement ring was inside. How could I say no?

We decided to live in San Diego, which meant that I now had to undo almost everything I had worked so hard to accomplish. I needed to sell my house that I had bought on my own, leave my good friends, and resign from my job as vice president. What was I thinking?!

I remember walking into the president's office to tender my resignation. He looked up from his desk and said, "Are you kidding me? What are you going to do, move to San Diego and become Betty Crocker?" I was stunned, upset at his obviously inappropriate comment, and a bit worried that he might be right.

Once in San Diego, I decided to take some time off before I started job hunting. I set to work planning our wedding, taking tennis lessons, going to the gym, lying in the sun, reading books—and pretty much going crazy with a lack of purpose. During a restless night's sleep, an idea for a new company came to me, and while leisurely sipping my coffee the next morning, I decided to write my business plan.

Sitting at my computer in the guest room, typing away, I was determined to finish my business plan before my wedding that was two weeks away. My stomach was queasy, and I just couldn't focus. I called my best friend and described my symptoms. She squealed with delight and said, "Go to the drugstore *right now*, get a pregnancy test, and pee on the stick!"

Whenever Morgan and I are looking through the photo albums, the same question always comes up: "Why wasn't I at your wedding, Mommy?" Under his breath, Mark mumbles like clockwork, "Technically, you *were*."

# Our Scars Make Us Stronger

There's a bit more to the whirlwind romance story that I just described. Actually, a lot more. I was in New York on September 11, 2001. It was a day that will forever be remembered by our country, and it was also two days after my first date with Mark. I don't know if it was fate or pure chance that I was sick in my hotel room when the first plane hit the World Trade Center instead of me being at a meeting less than half a mile away. I will never completely comprehend that truly awful day, but I do know that it rocked me to my core, and I am eternally grateful that I eventually made it back to California four days later.

As I began to reflect on the horrifying experience, I started to realize a dramatic change in my life view and priorities. Before that day, I had been relatively content being an independent, career-driven workaholic. After 9/11, I realized I wanted more. More true meaning in my life, more balance, and less concern for things that were ultimately unimportant.

Within six months, my life took a 180-degree turn as I got engaged, sold my home, resigned from my job, and moved to San Diego. I look back at that time, and although I'm still a little shocked about all the coinciding drastic changes, I know that they were the right choices. I believe that all of us have pivotal moments in our lives when we choose our course. We can opt to stay in our comfort zones (or sometimes uncomfortable zones), or we can take a leap of faith and find our true path.

Many authors and speakers talk about overcoming challenges and allowing failures to propel us forward. I believe that rather than the obstacles themselves, it's how you chose to conquer them. When I was twelve years old and in the midst of that horrible time called middle school, I was diagnosed with scoliosis. My parents took me to a renowned back specialist who was on the cutting edge of experimental treatments during that time. Our hope was to prevent the spine curvature from getting worse and keep my state-ranked gymnastics career intact.

Unfortunately, the preliminary treatments were not effective, and the only option was major back surgery. They scheduled the treatment during my eighth-grade year. Although that is an incredibly awkward stage for most girls (and I think I took the cake), I somehow still felt that I would make it out on top. My doctor had explained that the recovery would last for weeks and had outlined all of my future limitations. I pondered all of his declarations and in turn said, "That may be what happened for your other patients, but I am going to be the fastest recovering patient you've ever had!" And I was.

I wholeheartedly believe that my positive outlook was paramount in my record-setting recovery, but even the best attitude can't prevent you from being human. Not long after the surgery, my mom and I went bathing suit shopping. I started to cry in the dressing room at the sight of the six-inch scar along my spine. No amount of coaxing could get me to come out. When I finally redressed and emerged, I asked my mom, "Will anyone ever love me with my scar?"

What I've learned as I've gotten older is that we all have scars—some are physical, but most psychological. They are the things in life that hold us back, that create doubt and make us think that we aren't good enough. But we're better than good enough, and we're stronger than we know.

My scar to me is now a symbol of my strength, a part of my journey, and one of the reasons I am who I've become. I'm a fighter, an eternal optimist (to a fault), and I don't take no for an answer. When someone asks me now, "What happened to your back?" I simply say, "I have a metal rod in my back, and I'm the bionic woman. I can take on anything!"

# The Myth of Mommyhood

"Being a mom is the best job you'll ever have" is a quote frequently shared between women. I agree 100 percent, but it should also be said that "being a mom is the hardest job you'll ever have." For most of us moms, having children is a dream that we have wished for since we were little girls playing with our dolls. Wasn't it fun to dress them up in pretty little dresses, pretend we were feeding them, and then rock them to sleep? Such peaceful little creatures! The thought of being a mommy brought up images of idyllic bliss and a sense of real completion and harmony in a family. Even the images of childbirth that we saw on TV were sheer perfection. A few pushes, and the doctor says, "It's a girl! (or boy)," and then he lays a perfectly clean little cherub on your chest. The reality of being a mom, starting with childbirth is, well, *messy*.

I have some darling, young, single women who work for me in my office. They often tell me how cute my kids are and how much they hope to have great children like mine someday. I realize every time I talk with them that there is an unspoken code between moms that you don't share the gory details of childbirth with untainted future moms. I find that I typically say something like, "It's an amazing experience. Giving birth is very hard, but once you have that beautiful little baby in your arms, you would do it again in a hot second." Followed by, "My only advice is, just don't bring pretty new pajamas with you to the hospital like they recommend in childbirth class, because all you really need are some baggy black sweats."

Being a mom is definitely an emotional roller coaster. It's amazing how fast you can go from happy to terrified to angry to just plain exhausted. When Morgan was about two and a half, she was upstairs in her room for naptime. I went up to check on her about twenty minutes into her nap and found that she wasn't in her room. Puzzled, I started to call her name. No answer. I began to go from room to room upstairs, looking for her, but she was nowhere to be found. Mild panic started to kick in. By this point I started running around the house yelling her name and looking in every corner, under every bed, and anywhere I could think of.

I was about thirty seconds away from calling the police when I decided to go back into her room one more time. I'm not sure what possessed me, but I opened the door to her closet, and there she was, curled up in a little ball, sleeping peacefully on the floor. I collapsed in the middle of her room and wept. Relief, frustration, and sheer unimaginable love for my daughter filled me to the core.

I've always been a strong-willed person, but I never realized how protective I could be until I became a mom. My husband refers to me as Mama Bear, and he knows to duck and cover when someone does something that upsets or hurts my kids. At Dylan's first "real" soccer game when he was just four years old, he was very intimidated because he was the youngest player on the field. As the game got started, it was clear that there was a player on the other team who was a bully; he kept pushing the smaller players around.

As a sports fan, I don't have a problem with players being aggressive, but I do think that you need to correct bad behavior when kids are young. Sure enough, during a throw in from the sidelines, this boy, with full force, pushed my son so hard that he went flying in the air and landed on his back, which knocked the wind out of him. I flew out of my chair, went running to my injured son, and started screaming at the referee to get control of the situation.

The coach from the other team (who happened to be a friend of my husband's unbeknownst to me), started screaming, "Sit down, Mom!" I proceeded to totally lose it.... It wasn't my proudest moment, but as most mothers understand, there isn't anything we wouldn't do to protect our kids.

From the second our children are born—actually it's really from the time they're conceived—there is a love and a bond like no other. I never used to understand when mothers would say "I would throw myself in front of a bus to save my child." I understand now. Being a mom is definitely different from what I'd expected. The love for our children is greater, the difficult times are harder, and it's very clear that none of us moms know what we're doing, but at all times we want the very best for our children.

# Me First

Remember back to kindergarten when the biggest drama of the day was when Suzy "cut" in line. It was so unfair. Why did *she* always get to be first? It almost goes without saying, but we as moms rarely allow ourselves to be first anymore. I mean really, can we in good conscience put ourselves before our husbands, our careers, our kids? The answer is *yes*. But before you close this book, saying that this is unrealistic, hear me out a little bit longer.

By putting yourself first, I don't mean living an unproductive life of leisure. When I think about "me time," I usually think about doing something indulgent, like going to the spa–a treat that's expensive, time-consuming, and ultimately, guilt-inducing. In the real world version of "me time," I'm referring to taking care of your well-being, your body, and your self-esteem.

Let's get it over with and talk about our weight first. For starters, almost all women I talk with have anxiety about their bodies. Ever since I can remember, I wanted to be skinnier. What woman doesn't? Even my best friend in high school who was five foot two and 102 pounds would comment on how "fat" she was. *Whatever!* When I was in my twenties, I was living the life of the Simply Super Single Woman; I would get up at 5 a.m. and head to my spin class followed by more cardio and some weight training. I'd head to work, put in a full day, and then join my friends for a margarita (or two or three) at happy hour. Ahhh, just thinking about those days makes me nostalgic. Looking back, I looked pretty good, but I remember never being happy with my body and always vowing to fit into a smaller pair of jeans.

Then you get pregnant...*gulp!* I wish I was one of those woman who loved being pregnant. We've been told our whole life that having a baby is what our body was meant to do. Maybe I am just really vain, but after I had been working for years trying to keep everything toned, tight, and in check, watching my body grow into a large beach ball wasn't really my favorite thing. I think that the "in-between stage" was the hardest. This is the time when you have become thick around the middle and puffy, and not a single pair of pants fit around your waist.

Around this glorious time, my husband and I were getting ready to head out to dinner with friends (remember when you could do that?), and I exclaimed in despair that I had absolutely nothing to wear. All of my maternity clothes were still too big, and none of my regular clothes (even my "fat" jeans) would fit. My husband, who is six foot two and 210 pounds, suggested from across the hall, "Honey, why don't you just wear a pair of my jeans." I'm sure that you can picture the ensuing meltdown. "I can't go out....I'm so fat....I'm never going to get my body back!" Bless his heart, I know that he was only trying to help, but I was tempted to contact a divorce attorney.

Pregnancy is really just the warm-up for what is to come when our little babies make their appearance in the real world. Our worlds get rocked even more after the baby is born. Our bodies become milk-factories and refuse to let go of those extra pounds.

A few weeks after Morgan was born, I was driving home from a business meeting and was feeling quite proud of myself for finding a way to balance work and motherhood. As I drove down the freeway, I suddenly heard whistling and cat-calling coming from the car next to me. I casually looked over, and four college-aged boys were desperately trying to get my attention. I heard one of them shout, "Hey, nice boobs!" (although he used a different nickname for them). I was torn between being really flattered, since my boobs *were* the biggest they'd ever been, and being completely mortified because their sole purpose now was making food.

From the time we find out we're expecting, we receive all kinds of advice from friends, doctors, and of course total strangers on how to keep our bodies in check. "Make sure you eat enough." "Don't eat too much." "Be sure to continue to exercise." "Don't exercise too much!" It's enough to make your head swim. What I realized very quickly both during pregnancy and afterward was that I felt better when I incorporated exercise and healthy eating into my day. It's not easy, and there are a million excuses we can use for why we can't do either one. When it comes down to it, though, aren't we happier as individuals, moms, and wives when we feel good about ourselves?

And what about our emotional well-being? This one can be even harder to tackle because it's not a simple formula. I've found that there are a few tricks to getting out of the emotional rut that we moms find ourselves in on a regular basis.

The first is to find an activity or hobby that's just for you and doesn't involve your husband or significant other, or your kids. Every woman has different interests, but this could mean taking an art or drama class, signing up for an adult sports league, or volunteering for a cause that's close to your heart. Most importantly, you need to make time for this activity because it's *your* time.

Second, find ways to mix up your daily routine. Having a family schedule can be good for kids, but it can also end up making moms stagnant. To prevent this from happening, add some variety into your daily tasks, such as trying new recipes or mixing up your workout regime. Adding a little creativity to these everyday responsibilities can make them much more interesting.

Finally, be sure to incorporate adult time into your life. This could be catching up with your girlfriends or going on a date with your significant other. As much as we all love our children, we need time away from them. During your adult time, it's important to talk about things other than your kids. If you find that you don't have anything to talk about, refer back to the two paragraphs above, and make some changes.

You need to decide that you *deserve* to take care of yourself. *No excuses!* If it means getting up an hour early to exercise before the kids wake up, so be it. If you need to pay twelve dollars an hour for a babysitter so you can have your adult or "me" time, it will be money well spent. No, it's not easy to find time for your personal well-being, so you must create time in your schedule. You may end up with a little less sleep (what mom really sleeps anyways?), but, believe me, your newfound confidence and positive attitude will make up for it.

# Be Perfectly Imperfect

If there was a "Worst Mother of the Day" award, I'm sure I would qualify for the prize on a regular basis. I'm not sure if this sounds familiar, but here's how I sometimes see a typical weekday:

1. Get out of bed ten minutes late after pressing the snooze button—*so tired!*
2. Quick workout (never long enough) followed by scrambling to get showered and dressed. Change outfits three times.
3. Get the kids ready for school. Can't find new Skechers. Dylan's jeans are too short. Kids eat frozen waffles; no fruit or anything remotely healthy.
4. Pick up carpool (five minutes late). Yell at kids for yelling in the car. Drop kids off at school and realize I forgot to pack their snacks.

5. Drive back to school to deliver snacks.
6. Unsuccessfully try to cram ten hours' worth of work into six hours.
7. Drive kids to soccer practice (I mean, speed to soccer practice). Arrive five minutes late.
8. Go to McDonald's drive-through on the way home. Don't buy the Happy Meals (a rip-off), but buy from the dollar menu instead, which makes the kids mad.
9. Homework, reading log, showers, practice singing for voice lessons....
10. Lie in bed. Can't sleep, thinking about all the things I screwed up today.

It's so easy to remember every single thing we've done wrong during the course of the day, but rarely do we give ourselves credit for the things we do right. What if we were to look at the positive side of our parenting instead of just beating ourselves up for everything we do wrong? The same day could look something like this:

1. Get out of bed (an accomplishment in itself).
2. Work out. Feels great to get that out of the way in the morning!
3. Kids are self-sufficient and get themselves ready in the morning. Dylan's clothes are getting small, so make note to go shopping this weekend.
4. Drive kids to school. Dylan blows me a kiss good-bye. Makes my whole day.

5. Realize I forgot the kids' snacks and feel good that I brought them to school later so the kids wouldn't be hungry.
6. Get lots of work done. Check seventeen items off my to-do list.
7. Take kids to soccer practice. A great way to incorporate physical activity into their day.
8. Hit the drive-through on the way home. Skip the French fries, and serve their cheeseburgers with fruit and milk at dinner.
9. Spend time together helping with homework and teaching the kids about responsibility and preparing for their upcoming day.
10. Share a special moment with each child as I tuck them into bed. Go to bed knowing I did my best.

Accepting our imperfections is definitely difficult. Some days it's easier than others. Ultimately, we need to learn to forgive ourselves when we make mistakes and correct our course when necessary.

Both of my kids are playing their first year of competitive soccer, which is a new experience for our family. My husband and I are competitive people by nature, and it seems that the other players also have "spirited" parents. My son's team has been a challenge for many reasons, including a brand-new coach who isn't yet confident in her abilities, along with some very inexperienced players on the team who shouldn't be playing at this level.

All things combined, the poor boys had a 0-8 season, which was frustrating for everyone involved. During a particularly tough game (the score was 0-13 when I stopped counting), I found myself screaming directions at Dylan from the sidelines since the coach wasn't providing instructions on what to do. In the middle of the game, Dylan came running off the field, crying, and said, "Mommy, *please* stop yelling at me!"

In that moment, I felt like the worst parent on the planet. I knew I was wrong, but I couldn't take it back. The realization that I had pushed my son too far and put too much importance on a silly soccer game snapped me back into reality. I'm still trying to forgive myself for that moment, but I'm doing my best to move forward and put everything in perspective. We as moms make tons of mistakes—some will be little and others may have a bigger impact on our children. The best we can do is acknowledge that we are imperfect, teach our children the art of saying "I'm sorry" when we're wrong, and live life with good intentions, knowing that we'll make mistakes again.

If we look hard enough, we can find some redeeming qualities in our imperfect moments. At the park one afternoon, Morgan, who was three at the time, was playing beautifully in the sandbox with one of her preschool friends. Because she is my firstborn, it was hard not to be a "helicopter" mom, but I was doing a pretty good job of letting her have her own space. I finally gave in to my meddling tendencies and went over to see what she was building. "Look, Mom," she said, "I'm making Mount Kilimanjaro! Did you know that it's in Tanzania?"

The first thing I did when I got home was take Morgan over to the globe and ask, "Can you show Mommy where Tanzania is?" I wasn't testing her....I really had no idea where it was. I continued to be perplexed as to how she could possibly have known this information until I later realized she had learned it from Dora the Explorer on TV. This proved to me that television really *does* make a good babysitter once in a while.

The bottom line is that we don't give ourselves enough credit for the things we do right. If our best intentions end up going wrong, we can correct our course along the way. Each evening, even if the day didn't go your way, try to find at least one thing that made you proud. If that's hard to do, remember that tomorrow is another day, and get ready to *rock it!*

# Embrace Change-or at Least Don't Fight It

On a regular basis, my husband tells me how stubborn I am. I'll admit, I *am* pretty stuck in my ways and definitely want what I want. Not in a spoiled brat kind of a way, but in a determined-to-do-things-right kind of way. I'd like to argue with him about it, but he's equally as stubborn as I am (although he would never admit to it). My one consolation is that my daughter has inherited it from both of us, which means she has a double dose of the stubborn gene. I can't wait until the teenage years...oh joy.

For us bullheaded folk, change is a hard thing to embrace. Just when things are seemingly running smoothly, all of a sudden something happens to throw everything into a tailspin. Life comes at lightning speed, and the necessity of change can come in many forms:

- Things in life aren't going well, and you need to make adjustments
- A crisis occurs, and you're forced to adapt
- Your world is going pretty smoothly, but you're getting too comfortable and need to make adjustments

I can remember not long ago when my business was being hard hit by the downturn in the economy. I'm a competitor by nature, so I wasn't about to throw in the towel after so many years of hard work, but I felt my inner fight slowly diminishing with each passing day. Not only did I feel the impact in my work, but the blow to my self-esteem took its toll in my personal and family life as well. After a few weeks of being depressed, I decided that I had two options: (1) evolve my business or (2) give up. Since choice number two wasn't an option, I focused on creating a new division in my company that would prosper in the new reality we were living in.

The word that I like to use even more than *change* is *evolve*. *Change* implies doing a complete adjustment of your course, while *evolve* means that you can leverage all of your past experience and convert that knowledge into something new. There are certainly times in our lives where we need a real change—a new relationship or career, a move to a new city, or maybe just a sassy new haircut to spice things up a bit. But even in these moments of real change, we are pulling from our life experiences and can choose our future course based on our knowledge of the past.

A few years back, one of my closest friends said, "Why are you always so lucky?" Although I have been fortunate to have a good upbringing and foundation, I was actually a bit offended by her statement. I've always lived my life with strong convictions and a nonstop work ethic. I've worked like a dog for my "luck." The way I see it, life is a lot less about luck (although certainly that comes into play from time to time) and a lot more about how you navigate life's uncertainties.

You will never be "lucky" if you don't put yourself in the position to broaden your horizons and explore new things. When you walk into a room of new people, make yourself approachable, be open-minded, and join conversations. Chance meetings with new people can turn into opportunities if you take the lead in building a relationship. When you're passionate and have a vision, go for it! And when you're tired of the "pity party" that comes with disappointments, decide that you *choose* to be a success—and make it happen.

Even in good times, getting too comfortable is never a good thing. I've found that when you get out of your comfort zone and push yourself to find new experiences, you almost always grow as a person. When my husband and I were house hunting after Morgan's birth, we hired Jerry, a realtor we met in one of the open houses we visited. Jerry's favorite saying was, "You miss 100 percent of the shots you don't take." After about the twentieth time we heard this quote, it became an ongoing joke between Mark and me.

Laughing aside, that quote does have some merit. As moms, we all have dreams and ambitions, but most of us are too scared to pursue them. I'm certainly not recommending becoming an irresponsible parent and making bad choices, but it's okay to put yourself out there. Sure, you may fail, and you'll definitely hear more than one *no* along the way. But what *if* you push yourself and decide to follow that dream? You just might end up getting what you want.

# Believe in Your Self-Worth

When Dylan was a kindergartener, he announced at the dinner table that he had a girlfriend. As most mothers would do, I asked, "Does she know that she's your girlfriend?" He looked at me confidently and said, "When I told her she was my girlfriend, she gave me a big hug." It sounds like she approved.

Now, as a mom who is certain that there will never be anyone good enough for my only son, I have to say that I was pleased by his choice of girlfriends. Not only did she live only three houses away (cuts down on the gas expense), but she was also well-mannered, smart, and had an adorable fashion sense.

After school one day, Dylan told me he wanted to buy her some flowers. To be frugal, I suggested that picking flowers from our backyard would make them even more special. After we collected our bouquet, we walked the half-block to her house and knocked on her door to present the heartfelt token of his adoration. When Dylan handed the flowers to her, a huge grin came over her face—my son had helped her to feel valued and cherished. What a wonderful gift!

Just when I thought Dylan couldn't get any sweeter, he gave me a present called Mom's Box. He put it next to my bed, and every night he wrote a little note telling me the things he loved about me. I have kept every single one of those notes, because they provide a ray of hope on those days when I feel like life has chewed me up and spit me out. To know that I'm loved and valued does amazing things to restore my self-worth.

My son's beautiful notes are a treasure for sure, but it's equally important to believe in my self-worth from within. I find that as I get older, it gets easier to find more and more flaws in myself: my crow's feet are getting more prominent, my temper flares easier, and I forget everything unless it's written down in my Outlook calendar (and even then I sometimes still screw up).

It's easy to go through our mommy years feeling lost if we don't find a way to meaningfully contribute and to create a sense of accomplishment. Take time to set your own goals and "create" time to achieve them. It's really easy to say, "I'm a mom and I don't have time to do things for myself."

We tend to put everybody else first and create excuses as to why we can't fulfill our dreams and aspirations.

And sometimes we don't even know what it is that we really need for ourselves. I found myself in this exact situation when I was transitioning from super single woman to suburbanite after my engagement to Mark. I was going through a complete identity crisis, so I decided to seek help from a life coach.

Now, some of you make think that a life coach isn't a real therapist, but I'll tell you that it was probably the best money I ever spent. My coach, John, had me do an exercise that I still remember to this day. He said, "I want you to make a list of every job you would be interested in having. And *don't* censor yourself, even if it seems ridiculous." I went home that evening and started making my list. It included CEO, mom, event planner, news anchor, business owner, magazine publisher, wife, and of course, movie star.

I didn't realize it at the time, but I was putting all those things out into the universe and allowing them to be acknowledged. I can't say that the movie star part will likely happen, but wouldn't you know, the company that I ended up founding incorporates most of the other elements. I'm now a mom and wife who runs a company that publishes event-planning magazines and appears frequently on TV. *Who would have thought*? I have since realized that I'm the CEO of my own destiny, and the only one who can stand in my way is *me*.

So, what about setting a goal in your everyday life? The first step is to find one. What have you been wanting or meaning to do and have been putting off? Running a half marathon? Losing your baby weight? Taking an art class? Getting your MBA?

Once you've established your goal and timeline, hold a family meeting at the dinner table and discuss your plans. Once everyone is onboard, set the wheels in motion to start your journey. This may take some initial coordination, including hiring babysitters, waking up earlier than usual, and setting up carpools. It should also include delegating age-appropriate responsibilities that will help your schedule keep moving in the right direction. This one is especially hard for me, because I'm convinced my husband is not capable of packing a lunch correctly or creating a perfectly-perky ponytail to complement my daughter's outfit, and I'm pretty sure he doesn't even know what time school starts. With a little training, and a lot of letting go, your family can work together as a team to create a new routine that includes your personal goals.

And guess what. Now that you've coordinated your schedule, it's time to follow it. If you've picked the right kind of activity, not only will you feel a tremendous sense of accomplishment when you achieve your goal, but you'll enjoy the journey along the way.

That's not to say that your ego and self-esteem won't take a few knocks along the way. A few weeks back, I was

From Margaritas to Mac 'n Cheese Mom

vigorously working out in my home gym, and Morgan came in and asked me to teach her some exercises. In the middle of our "training session," she said, "You know, Mom, your butt kind of jiggles like JELL-O. But I think you're perfect anyways!" Oh well, good thing I'm learning to accept myself, jiggles and all.

# Set Your Own Boundaries

I've heard that people get more and more set in their ways as they get older. None of us really likes to say no to people, but I've found that it's starting to get easier with age. "No, you can't play video games until your homework is done." "No, you can't eat that candy before dinner." "No, I'm not able to bake a cake for the school bake sale tomorrow."

I've never had a problem with confrontation. I guess it can be looked at as a blessing or a curse. That said, I think we all still have a desire to be liked and not to disappoint our friends and loved ones. One afternoon, Dylan asked me the day before his school trip to the aquarium, "Mommy, are you going to drive to the field trip?"

"I'm so sorry, honey," I said, "but Mom has to go to some meetings for work."

"Are you *ever* going to drive to one of my field trips?" he said as his eyes welled up with tears. I so hated to disappoint him, I rearranged my schedule to make sure I could drive to the next field trip.

With adults, however, I find that I'm not quite as understanding anymore. There's a fine line between relying on each other and taking advantage. At Morgan's last birthday party, one of her friends needed to stay about thirty minutes late because her parents had other obligations that afternoon. At the time, I was happy to do it, but when her parents showed up two hours after the party was over (without calling), I was not pleased.

This same mother called me a few days later and said that she had an "opportunity" for me to have her daughter over to *our* house for a play date after school. An opportunity? The afternoon in question happened to be an extremely busy one for us, so I proceeded to give her every reason I could think of why it wasn't going to work: it wasn't my day for carpool, my parents were in town, Dylan had soccer practice, I had work commitments, and on and on.

But all I really needed to say was, "I'm sorry, tomorrow just isn't a good day for us. Let's put another day on the calendar for the girls to get together." As my husband and I talked before bed that night, he didn't understand why I was so upset. I tried to explain to him that is was pretty simple. Saying *no* equals guilt.

I'm learning, slowly but surely, to establish my own personal boundaries. If you're having trouble saying no to all of the requests that come your way, consider making a quick list of your top priorities to help keep your focus. Here's my personal list:

- My children
- My husband
- My health
- My friends and family
- My company and career
- My home
- My community

Even a short list can be filled with "opportunities" that you'll need to pass up. The trick is to listen to your gut with each potential responsibility that comes your way. If your heart starts beating faster and you feel your stress level rising before you've even committed, it probably means you're taking on too much. Just remember that it *is* okay to say no sometimes. If you overcommit, you'll end up feeling resentful and find it hard to meet your obligations. You'll ultimately be more successful if you're honest with yourself about what you can take on and if you do a great job with the projects you select. Not only will you be helping those who are the most important to you, you'll also end up with a greater sense of accomplishment and well-being.

I think it would be remiss not to talk about boundaries with technology as well. We live in a time when smartphones, computers, iPads, video games, and TV are around us constantly. I find myself daily saying, "Morgan and Dylan, turn off the Wii. No more TV for the day. Get off of the computer." Isn't it interesting, though, that while I'm shouting these things at the kids, I'm usually in the process of returning a text message on my Blackberry or sending *one last* email before I shut the computer down for the day. I'm certainly not going to preach going without your technology, but I do feel that we need to set boundaries between our tech time and our family time. Here are a few rules I try to live by:

- Turn off the computer at the end of the workday. If you absolutely need to get a few more things done, do it after the kids are in bed and set a firm time limit.
- Don't put your cell phone next to your bed at night. I keep mine downstairs. It's too easy to be sucked in by the flashing red light letting you know that yet another email, text, or call has come in.
- When you're enjoying personal time with your family or friends, let voicemail answer your calls. Not every call or text needs to be responded to immediately; sometimes people just need to wait.
- Don't put your cell phone number on your business card unless you really want to be called *anytime*. I give my cell phone number only to family, friends, and business associates who will use it respectfully.

We all need to establish our own boundaries that work for our individual lifestyles. Don't make apologies, and definitely lose the guilt. Ultimately people will respect you more when you're honest and direct with them, and you'll find a greater sense of balance when you're confident in your choices.

# Be in Your Moment

Isn't there an expression about the "best laid plans"? Being from San Diego, my children had never seen snow. Not one single snowflake. For a lot of people this may not seem like a big deal, but since my little ones had been saying, "Mommy, how come it doesn't snow in San Diego?" and "When can we make snow angels?" I thought it was time to make the trek to the local mountains to find the fluffy white stuff. We decided to drive up to Big Bear to celebrate Dylan's third birthday. What could be more magical than having snow falling on your birthday when you're a Southern California boy?

We packed up the car with the two kids, the dog (did I mention that we had recently rescued a dog from the local shelter?), our cold-weather gear, and of course, lots of snacks. About twenty minutes into our road trip, our dog proceeded to throw up all over the floor mat in the front seat. *Nice.* A quick stop at the gas station and we were back on our way.

Things were moving along beautifully until we started driving up the winding mountainside. Within five minutes of each other, the dog vomited again and Morgan, who had been saying that her "tummy didn't feel good," had a projectile throw-up like I've never seen before in my life. She was crying, the dog was shaking, and Dylan was saying, "Mommy, *when* are we going to get there? This is not fun!" *Good times!*

As if things hadn't been going bad enough, we spent the first two days holed up in our cabin because it was pouring rain. That's right, rain—and not a speck of snow. We were all going stir crazy in our tiny little red cabin.

On the last morning of our trip, I woke up before everyone else and said a little prayer in my head "Please, please let it snow. Just a little bit." I peeked through the blinds, and to my disbelief, I saw a few small snowflakes starting to fall. And they kept coming. I ran into the kids' room and gently nudged them awake. "It's snowing. It's really snowing!" I said.

Morgan and Dylan hurried to put on their mittens, jackets, and hats over their pajamas, and we ran outside. The sheer joy on their faces made all the hiccups of the past few days fade away. We had seen the snow together as a family and created a lifetime memory.

 From Margaritas to Mac 'n Cheese Mom

This is the good stuff. The part of life that's *really* important. If there's one thing that I've learned as a mom it's to take a few minutes each week and write down the kids' milestones, funny sayings, and things they'll want to remember later in life. I keep a journal for each of them, and they've come in handy while I was writing this book. A common thread that I've found while reading back through them is that it's times we have spent together as a family that have been the most meaningful and created the funniest and most memorable moments.

Frequently, opportunities for "the good stuff" seem to come at inopportune times. "Mom, can you play LEGOs with me?" Dylan asked at 7:40 on a school night.

"Sure honey, in a few minutes," I said. What I really meant was, "Probably not, honey, because Mom still needs to wash the dishes, pack your lunches, check your homework, make coffee for tomorrow, set out your clothes, get everyone ready for bed, and...collapse."

Because of my false promise, Dylan kept asking throughout the evening, and I continued to disappoint him. I'm not advocating dropping everything all the time, but I decided one night to put my to-dos on hold and go have a short LEGO-building party with Dylan. He showed off his many creations (quite impressive), and we made up stories with his mini-figures and rearranged the city that he had so diligently built on his train table.

I realized two things in that moment: (1) I'm a terrible LEGO builder, and (2) my son was glowing. It took just fifteen minutes to bring us together, and somehow the other stresses of the day seemed to fade away. In our hectic schedules, sometimes all it takes to get us back to our center is to *stop*...and take in the moment.

And sometimes the memorable moments come at the least expected times. As I set the table for Thanksgiving dinner a few years back, I asked Morgan, who was three at the time, if she knew what Thanksgiving was all about. "Of course, Mom," she chirped, "Thanksgiving is when you give all of your Halloween candy back!" Close...so close.

A few years later, we were opening our Christmas cards, and I showed one of them to Dylan, who had just turned four. It was from my sister and had a picture of my newborn nephew. "Do you know who this is?" I asked Dylan.

"Well," he said hesitantly, "it's either Cousin Bradley or baby Jesus." One out of two isn't bad!

# **Simplify**

The company that I started during my pregnancy is called Party Plan-It, Inc. Because of the name, most people think I actually plan parties, but the truth of the matter is, we're the "matchmakers" between the clients and the locations and vendors. I'm definitely not an expert event planner, a décor specialist, or a chef.

This confusion, however, has led to me being nominated every year in my kids' classrooms as class party mom. The conversation usually goes something like this:

"Deborah, since you're an event planner, could you be the party mom for our class?"

"Well, I'm not actually a party planner but I—"

"Perfect, I can't wait to see what incredible ideas you come up with!"

*No pressure!* I've spent many hours scouring the internet to find out how to make tissue-paper hearts and find the rules for Pass the Pumpkin. With certain moms in the class, I've found that this party planning is actually more of a sport, and there are clear winners and losers. And yes, they *are* keeping score.

After school one day in first grade, Morgan came home and said, "Abbey's mom brought in cupcakes for her birthday, and each one had a face that looked *just* like the kid she was giving it to. Mine had blond hair, blue eyes, and freckles, just like me!" This was followed by "How come you always buy my birthday cupcakes at the grocery store?" *Ouch.* As usual, I started tallying up all my inadequacies in my head.

The same pressures can be felt for kids' birthday parties. When did throwing a five-year-old's birthday party start to become a competition?

I've realized a few truths after many years of being the party mom:

1. Kids prefer things to be simple (and so do the teachers).
2. Most kids don't eat much anyway, so don't obsess about the food.
3. If you think that a craft or game might be too complicated, it is.

4. Don't try to do it all yourself. Delegate.

And for the moms who enjoy spending three days working on decorations for the kindergarten spring party—knock yourself out! Just remember that you're really doing it for yourself. Your kids are just happy that you were able to attend and excited not to be doing school work for a change.

Parties aside, have you ever noticed that we parents try to make things much more complicated than they need to be? When kids are little, they're more fascinated with the wrapping paper than the actual present. In our quest to be perfect parents, we often forget that it's the simple things in life that are the most meaningful.

This past summer, we decided to do a combo vacation that included a few days at Disney World in Orlando, followed by a three-night cruise to the Bahamas. Our kids were finally at the right age where they could be in camp part of the time on the cruise ship so we could enjoy both family and adult time.

Of course, it poured rain our entire stay in Orlando. We still visited the theme parks in our rain parkas from morning until night and spent hundreds of dollars on hotels, park tickets, food, souvenirs, and more. As we were leaving the hotel, the kids said, "I wish we had more time just to hang out and swim in the pool." The pool? What a simple concept.

Next stop was the cruise. Still raining, of course! The kids were in awe of the "floating hotel" and wanted to explore every single nook and cranny on the ship. As a general rule, I'm not a huge cruise person, as I can't eat nine meals per day, and smoky casinos aren't really my thing. That aside, it was a blast to have our family together, dancing on the pool deck and living in the moment.

One of the ports during the cruise was an island called Coco Cay, which is basically a huge beach. Between rainstorms, Mark and I found ourselves relaxing on lounge chairs while the kids played in the ocean for hours. They chased each other in the waves, collected hundreds of shells, and found hermit crabs to play with. In that moment, I realized that although we were on an amazing tropical island, it was the simple things that the kids were enjoying most. More than Disney, more than the cruise ship, a beach was all they needed to create their own magic.

It's easy to get caught up in life and feel pressure to outdo one another. The fact is, there is a lot of truth to the expression "Less is more."

I'd like to think of myself as a smart person, but I frequently look back at some of the parenting challenges I've encountered and wonder why I didn't see the obvious and simple answer that was right in front of me. I think this must be a common challenge we moms face, because I had a conversation with my sister about this exact subject just the other day. She was talking about how my future fashionista, two-year-old niece, Amanda, had started to take all her clothes and pajamas out of her drawers during naptime so she could try them all on. After each "nap," my sister would go into Amanda's room and reprimand her for taking everything out, and then she'd refold all of the clothes and put them away.

After many frustrating weeks of this routine, my sister realized that if she took Amanda's clothes out of her room, it wouldn't keep happening. Problem solved.

We moms tend to obsess and overthink most situations with the intention of being the best parents we can be. The reality is that we end up bringing a lot of unnecessary stress to ourselves. Sometimes if we just stop, breathe, and look for the simple answer, we can spend our time on more productive and fulfilling endeavors.

# We Are Better Together

As woman, we are a powerful group. We can create life. We are nurturers, leaders, and influencers. So why is it that we end up being most critical of each other? One of the great mysteries that has plagued me during my adult life is why we as woman can often be so mean-spirited and competitive with each other. I believe it has a tremendous amount to do with this journey that we share and our desperate attempt to find a piece of our true selves in our lives as mothers.

After my daughter was born, I was on a quest to become the perfect mom, wife, and entrepreneur. I had no idea what I was getting into with motherhood or my business. I vowed that I would find the ideal balance between mommy time and work-time. Although I didn't have maternity leave, since that's not part of the work-for-yourself program, I was proud of my multitasking capabilities. I would make phone calls during her nap time, email while she was nursing (it's amazing what you can do with a Boppy on your lap), and go running while she was in the jogging stroller.

As any good mother would do, I also joined a playgroup. (By the way, this is actually false advertising, because infants don't really "play" with each other.) I determined that playgroups were really a reason for moms to take a shower, change into clothes other than sweats, and get out of the house. My intention when I joined was to bond with other moms who were going through similar experiences and to allow Morgan to make some friends and interact with other little ones.

I attended the group faithfully every week but started to feel very insecure about myself after a few meetings. The topics of discussion always seemed to go along these lines: Are you still breastfeeding? What brand of diapers do you use? Do you make your baby food from scratch? I felt I was obviously not with the program, because I had started integrating baby formula into Morgan's feeding schedule (*gasp!*), bought whichever diapers were on sale at Target, and thought Gerber baby food was just fine—the baby on the label looked happy and healthy, after all.

I remember my last day of the playgroup like it was yesterday. We were all at a local park with our babies, and I mentioned to one of the other moms that, unfortunately, I needed to leave a little early to get back to the office. Her response was, "Ohhh, that's too bad that you *have* to work." The very next day, I emailed my resignation to the head of the playgroup.

What I realized in that moment was that, although I did *need* to work, I also *chose* to work. For me, being a working woman is part of my identity and an important part of my self-worth. I truly believe that each of us has unique gifts and abilities. I have often envied women who choose to stay at home with their children and seem to have infinite amounts of patience and creativity. What bothers me is when we as woman don't accept each other for our unique choices and, even worse, when we doubt ourselves.

As the kids got older, it also become clear that school has become more and more competitive and that parents were leading the charge. My family is fortunate to live in a suburb of San Diego that has very good public schools. Even in these times when education funding has been slashed terribly by the state, our teachers and families have been able to pull together to supplement the schools with additional funds, programs, and parent volunteers. In our community of high achievers, however, I find that there is a huge amount of competition, especially between the moms. I must admit that this is a phenomenon I've never fully understood. To me, we should all be given a medal for getting our kids to school on time with relatively clean clothes, completed homework in their backpacks, and a nutritious snack in hand (at least on most days).

It's time that we gave each other a break! Every mom I know is trying to find her balance. Our families' priorities and the ways we go about accomplishing things may be different, but we all are ultimately searching for the same thing—happiness. I would suggest that instead of judging each other, we open up and offer our friendship and help. By this I don't mean forcing unsolicited advice on unwilling recipients, but rather expressing your concern when you can tell a mom is having a hard day, offering assistance if you can take a load off her shoulders, or simply giving a reassuring smile across the room to show you understand. We as moms truly are better when we stick together. Life is hard enough; let's be kind to each other.

## Stay True to Yourself

The other morning, I was walking Dylan into school when one of his precocious little classmates came running up to me and chirped, "Good morning, Dylan's mommy!" It struck me that I no longer really have my own identity; instead my persona is intertwined with that of my children. Titles that I've inherited over the past few years include class party mom, team banner mom, and soccer mom, just to name a few. Many times I've perused the snack aisle at the grocery store deciding if I want to be the cool mom who brings chips and cookies at the end of the game or the healthy, a.k.a. boring mom who brings carrots and celery sticks.

Beginning with the moment we find out we are expecting a baby, our identity and responsibilities change drastically. As an avid coffee drinker (okay, coffee addict), it was almost unfathomable that I was supposed to cut out my cups of java every morning. And who doesn't enjoy a nice relaxing glass of wine at the end of a tough day. That had to go, too? Although refraining from some of these habits was a healthier choice anyway, it's amazing to realize how little habits become a big part your personality.

In the evolution from single life to mommyhood, it's easy to lose ourselves in our children. And although becoming a mother is the greatest responsibility we can take on, it's important to realize that being true to ourselves, our beliefs, and our passions will ultimately set the best example for our kids. In talking with many of my mommy friends, I frequently hear comments like, "I don't even know who I am anymore" and "When do I get time for me?"

I'm a firm believer that we need to recognize that our personalities are what make us unique and to find ways to incorporate our quirks and strengths into our parenting roles. When we're feeling a bit lost, thinking back to our preparenting days is a great way to remember some of our characteristics that make us who we are. As woman we can be many things:

- Nurturing
- Driven
- Athletic
- Sensitive
- Neurotic
- Organized

- Spontaneous
- Controlling
- Free-spirited
- Competitive
- Caring
- Perfectionists

I would describe myself as a driven, passionate, competitive, protective, and overly excitable perfectionist. As I've gotten older (although they say that forty is the new twenty, right?), I've realized two things: (1) as mothers, we must find ways to fulfill our personalities within our family lives, and (2) we need to learn to accept our imperfect selves.

Prior to being a wife and mother, I had a career that gave me the opportunity to travel the world and be a part of high-level negotiations on a regular basis. This tapped into many of my personality traits as I was driven to succeed and loved the thrill of the chase and of closing a challenging deal. After relocating to San Diego and resigning from my job, I felt extremely lost because I didn't have my normal sense of accomplishment.

After much soul searching, I decided to start my own company, and I realized that I could utilize my entrepreneurial spirit and determination to create my own destiny. When Morgan was born, I found that I also had a protective and nurturing side that was awakened, as only motherhood can do.

As my children continue to grow, I find that I can also embrace my character traits through their activities and pursuits. My competitive nature is one that certainly stands out on the sidelines of the soccer field (I really try just to yell positive encouragement). Teaching my children to always do their best allows me to serve as a mentor. Each of us as moms can fulfill our own needs by pursuing activities that allow us to be ourselves and to incorporate our strengths into our parenting style.

And most important, it's time that we moms give ourselves some credit and accept our limitations. Are we perfect? No. Will we make many mistakes? Definitely *yes!* Believe it or not, our children will be okay if we buy cupcakes at the grocery store rather than bake them from scratch until 3 a.m. It won't have a lasting impact if we miss one t-ball game because we have an evening business meeting. And if we end up in World War III after taking away video game privileges, this too shall pass—and will actually make them better, more responsible kids in the long run.

Be present in your own life and make a conscious decision to find the good each day. When you pause and enjoy life's littlest moments, you will fuel your soul, your heart, and your desire to pursue the things that make you complete as a woman and a mother.

I'll admit that every once in a while I still daydream about living a life of leisure—and yes, maybe eating a bonbon or two. But now I'm a mac 'n cheese mom (the kind from the box that is). And guess what. That's okay with me.

# Book Club Question Guide

1. What chapter could you relate to the most? Why?
2. What things did you give up when you became a mom?
3. If there was one thing you would like to do for yourself at this point in your life, what would it be?
4. What do you love the most about being a mom? What do you miss the most about single life?
5. Is motherhood what you thought it would be? If not, how is it different?
6. Do you think it's possible to balance your own goals with those of your family? How can you do that?

## About the Author

"Yes, you can have it all!" says Deborah Stumm. "That is, if you define 'all' as the things that are most important in your life." For Deborah, that includes family, friends, fitness, and growing her trifecta of businesses that include locally focused resources for event planners, brides, and moms. As a frequent guest on NBC, FOX, and CW, Deborah has been named the "family expert" with a wealth of knowledge and tips for moms, kids, and families.

Deborah is the founder of SuperMoms360.com, "The Busy Mom's Guide to Being Simply... Super!" which is the latest edition to her Party Plan-It, Inc., family of companies. Her current titles include wife to Mark, mommy of Morgan and Dylan (and two rescue dogs), and nonstop entrepreneur. Prior to her life in suburbia, Deborah traveled the world as the VP of Sales for a large consumer products company and has worked for startups and Fortune 500 companies.

www.ingramcontent.com/pod-product-compliance
Lightning Source LLC
Chambersburg PA
CBHW071744040426
42446CB00012B/2470